To Shepard Smith,
    Thank you for keeping south Mississippi in front of your viewers.
    You have made a difference in our recovery.

Sincerely, Karen Read
June 14, 2008

From
Manhattan
to
Mississippi

A New Yorker Falls in Love with the South

Daisy Karam-Read

QUAIL RIDGE PRESS
BRANDON, MISSISSIPPI

Printed in Canada

Cover and chapter-opening illustrations by Meredith Norwood

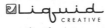

www.liquid-creative.com

Page illustrations by Carmen Fulford

Design by Cyndi Clark

Library of Congress Cataloging-in-Publication Data

Karam-Read, Daisy.
  From Manhattan to Mississippi : a New Yorker falls in love with the South / Daisy Karam-Read.
  p. cm.
  ISBN-13: 978-1-934193-09-9
  ISBN-10: 1-934193-09-7
  1. Mississippi—Social life and customs. 2. Ocean Springs (Miss.)—Social life and customs.
3. Southern States—Social life and customs. 4. Karam-Read, Daisy. 5. Ocean Springs (Miss.)—
Biography. 6. Manhattan (New York, N.Y.)—Biography. 7. New York (N.Y.)—Biography. 8.
Moving, Household—Social aspects—United States. 9. Moving, Household—United
States—Psychological aspects. 10. North and south. I. Title.
  F345.K37 2007
  304.8'762120747109049--dc22   2007027123

Second printing

QUAIL RIDGE PRESS
P. O. Box 123 • Brandon, Mississippi 39043
1-800-343-1583 • www.quailridge.com

In memory of my remarkable parents,
Stephan and Irmgard Karam,
and
for my husband, Jerry Read,
who has made all things possible for me

Contents

Preface

THIS BOOK IS A COLLECTION of personal observations on Mississippi and the Deep South from one who moved to Mississippi from New York City in 1998. They are candid reflections about the people and the things I've seen and heard and felt over the past nine years. My experiences in the Deep South have been humbling, sometimes startling, and always affecting.

A conversation with one who's never been to Mississippi usually begins with the assumption that everything and everyone there is decades behind the times, benightedly entrenched in the values of the antebellum South. I know this phenomenon well, because I was once just such a person. I would never have guessed, for example, that Mississippi was the first state to grant property rights to women (in 1839) or the first to maintain a state-supported college for women in 1884.

Living in Mississippi, however, yields a truer understanding. It's a state of enormous complexity, in which contradictions and ironies abound. Behind the Greek Revival columns, the southern drawl, and the "southern belle" and "Bubba" images, there are educated, well-read, sophisticated people, who are as open to new ideas as their big city cousins. They just don't sound and move like people from New York and Los Angeles.

The mindset of many people in other parts of the nation hasn't progressed beyond the tragic violence and indignities that white southerners perpetrated upon African Americans for too many years. Some northerners seem to have closed their minds about what it means to be a Mississippian today, holding on instead to the 1960s picture.

Mississippi's past includes institutional racism— there's no denying that—but I can honestly say that in nine years of living on the Mississippi Gulf Coast and spending a lot of time in New Orleans and other parts of Mississippi and Alabama, I have never witnessed a cruel act toward an African American nor heard an unkind comment. This is not to say that racial prejudice doesn't still exist here, but I've personally never encountered it.

On the contrary, I've been struck by how easily blacks and whites work together. I suppose that centuries of living alongside each other created a comfort level, or at least a familiarity, between the races that ironically may have helped them through the social transformation that's taken place in Mississippi since the 1960s. In other parts of the United States, there are probably still white people who've never even been alongside a black person in a supermarket line or a doctor's waiting room. I would have been unable to enjoy life in Mississippi if racism were a part of this psychology. In fact, I wouldn't have lasted one day, much less long enough to write this book.

It's time to update our thinking. In this slim volume I attempt to uncover the treasures of the state and its people and to share my discoveries with you. My comments are obviously subjective and impressionistic. They sometimes give way to generalizations—even politically incorrect ones. People in different parts of the country do fit into particular patterns, though I understand that by painting with a broad brush, I risk oversimplification and stereotyping. But this is not a scholarly social study.

When I draw an occasional comparison with New York or Los Angeles that sheds a less-than-flattering light on those great cities, I may provoke the ire of my fellow Northeast and West Coast citizens. My love for those metropolitan areas, which formed my greater consciousness, is undiminished and ongoing. Transplanting myself to Mississippi has enriched my life and given me a deeper understanding of this great country and its endless assortment of distinctive flavors.

Southern Attraction

"**Y**OU'RE MOVING TO MISSISSIPPI? You must be kidding me!" That was the response of my friends and colleagues when I announced that I'd fallen in love with a southern gentleman, after an impetuous courtship, and I was packing to move to a little town none of us had ever heard of—Ocean Springs, Mississippi, right on the Gulf of Mexico.

Those in my entire circle in New York and L.A. were in shock; they couldn't fathom that I would leave my beloved Manhattan, my apartment in Tribeca, and my bi-coastal lifestyle. I had been a struggling actress in New York and L.A. and felt equally at home on both coasts. Now I was working full-time in the cosmetics industry and traveling frequently from coast to coast. During one of my monthly business trips to Houston I met Barbara and Jimmie Lewis, a couple I liked immediately. Six months later,

Barbara said, "I have a man in mind for you." Because I trusted them, I agreed that Barbara could give Jerry my phone number. That was a life-changing moment; it was how I eventually met my husband.

Although I wasn't wealthy, my life thus far (June 1998) had held a measure of sophistication and glamour—Broadway shows, the Metropolitan Museum of Art, the New York Philharmonic, the Los Angeles Philharmonic, and other cultural events intrinsic to great metropolises. To an arts lover like me, it was an ideal existence, and I thrived on it. It would be an impossible adjustment, my companions said. I was the quintessential urbanite, and big city excitement was as necessary as oxygen for me. And I wasn't nineteen anymore; I was a woman of "a certain age."

"What will you do there?" my compatriots demanded to know. I was not domestic, had no interest in gardening, golf, or fishing, and I had never lived in any place smaller than a major metropolis. But I wasn't worried about finding things to do. I looked forward to exploring another part of the country.

JERRY READ and I were married on June 20, 1998, at Green Oaks Bed & Breakfast in Biloxi, Mississippi, in an intimate ceremony with only four people attending. The day was hot and still, and not a leaf stirred on the massive, ancient oaks. But it was beautiful and sunny, with a pristine sky poised over the Gulf, a lovely setting. Jerry had arranged the wedding, and the scene was redolent of the romance of the legendary Old South. Built in the early 1800s without the use of a single nail, Green Oaks was the perfect introduction to the traditional South—an exquisite architectural piece of south Mississippi's landscape, now part of my own personal history. On that sweltering day, we sat on the expansive verandah, with its old-fashioned swing, and "petticoat staircase" below. I imagined nineteenth century men ascending the stairs, sneaking a glimpse of the ladies' ankles as they floated up the facing staircase, petticoats slightly raised. At Green Oaks I sipped my first mint julep. The day following our nuptials, our wedding party set out for New Orleans for a Sunday jazz brunch at Commander's Palace, the white and turquoise Victorian restaurant in the Garden District. In this 1880 dining establishment, I enjoyed the best Bloody Mary I'd ever tasted. My new life had begun.

Since then, I've discovered much, and slowly shed my prejudices. I relinquished the provincialism of the intransigent New Yorker—an urbane provincialism, it's true, but narrowly regional nonetheless. One New Yorker at a luncheon counter on Lexington Avenue expressed her civic pride with these words: "When ya leave New Yawk, ya not going anywhere."

WAS MY ADJUSTMENT easy? No. Of course, I missed the newest exhibit at the Met, the evenings at Lincoln Center, the foreign films, and the chic boutiques within three minutes of my apartment. But it was an adjustment worth making, not only because I had married an exceptional man, but also because my vision expanded.

I DON'T KNOW if there was a single moment when I let go of the homesickness and embraced Mississippi. Perhaps it was that first spring, when, amazed by the sudden appearance of fuchsia azaleas in full bloom, I walked to my front yard mailbox. A sandy-haired boy about ten years old, straight out of a Norman Rockwell painting, was lying on the limb of a tree. Half obscured by the leaves, he eyed me with friendly curiosity. "Hi," he said, with a winning smile, not moving from his perch. I was disarmed. Coming upon a boy in this way may be nothing special to a rural Mississippian, but I had seen meetings like this only in Frank Capra movies.

My beguilement with the quirkiness of Mississippians, however, probably happened more gradually. I was surprised that the most accomplished Mississippians hold on to their earthy qualities. Some, even as adults, retain improbable childhood nicknames such as Doodles, Tootie, Fofo, Squattsy, Sankie, and Bootsie.

One unbearably hot June evening shortly before our wedding, Jerry's longtime friend Frank Hunger was coming to New Orleans, and we were looking forward to seeing him. A Mississippi native, he is a man of many achievements, and at the time was the head of the Civil Division of the Justice Department. Lean bodied and silver haired, Frank sauntered into Commander's Palace, reached into his jacket pocket, and said, "Daisy, I brought you some peppers from my yard." To my Yankee ears, it sounded like this: "Daisy, Ah brought you some peppahs from mah yawd." He then nonchalantly extracted the loose vegetables from his Saks Fifth Avenue suit—the modest, unaffected gesture of a Gary Cooper. A lack of pretense is one of the most engaging characteristics of Mississippians.

THE SOUNDS of Mississippi captivated me, too, like the plaintive whistle of the train that passed through Ocean Springs and across Biloxi Bay in the dark of night. So this was the sound that stirred the wanderlust of young people in isolated areas of this huge country, conjuring up images they had read about.

The melodic ancient Indian names charmed me. In times long past, the Biloxi (first people) spoke of the Yazoo (River of the Dead), the Escatawpa (Laughing Waters), and Pascagoula (the Singing River). The names were delightful to my ear.

I heard the legend of the Pascagoula River. The most famous of these tales describes the last chief of the Pascagoula tribe, who had lost all of his warriors in the deadly war with the Biloxi Indians. As the only surviving warrior of the last battle, with the enemy in relentless pursuit, he led the women and children, joining hands and singing, from the Pascagoula River to the sea, preferring the honor of death in the beloved waters to the shame and horror of captivity. Residents still claim to hear a mournful, otherworldly sound around midnight, although they can't predict exactly when it will occur. People say it's the song of death of the Pascagoula Indians' souls.

THOUGH I CAN'T IDENTIFY the precise time Mississippi insinuated itself into my soul, I do know this: no matter how genuinely southerners welcome the outsider—and Mississippians are truly inclusive—you never really become a part of the South. But the South becomes an indelible part of you.

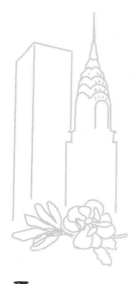

Simple Kindness

IF YOU NEEDED TO BORROW a lawnmower, how would you ask for it politely? In New York, you'd cut to the chase. You'd get on the phone and say, "John! Daisy. May I borrow your lawnmower?" In Mississippi, it's a production. You wander over to your neighbor's fence, talk for an hour about the weather, his family, politics, and as many other topics as either of you can think. Then you say, "Bah the way, may I borrow yo' lawnmower?"

In Mississippi, you ease into a topic. It seems impolite—even unfriendly—to ask for something outright. To southerners, there's crassness in getting right to the point. First, they want to show you they're happy to be in your company. This is the nature of manners in the Deep South—even for business transactions.

The word "charming" is so overworked that I hesitate to use it. Nonetheless, no other word so perfectly describes Ellis Branch, a popular Mississippi realtor. He's a charmer, whose appeal stems from a delightful sense of humor, well-bred manners, and an immense desire to please his clients. Originally from the Mississippi Delta where storytelling and good conversation are a social imperative and an art form, Ellis has one of those great southern male voices, the voice of a born raconteur.

One summer evening, he knocked at our door. I opened it to discover a tall, white-haired, elegantly casual man. My husband Jerry had asked him to come to discuss an inquiry we'd had from someone interested in purchasing our house. Ellis Branch and I had never met. Within minutes after his arrival, he commented admiringly on my accent. I replied in kind. As we walked the grounds and he looked at our house, we developed great rapport. In the course of an hour or so, I felt he'd become my friend. In fact, Ellis said that he liked us so much that he didn't want us to move. Later during the evening, he again insisted, "But you're *not* going to move." I'd never met a real estate agent who tried to talk me out of selling.

About a week later he asked us to join him for a glass of wine at Rudy's, the little clubhouse overlooking the golf course in Gulf Hills subdivision, where we lived at the time. The eponymous Rudy, a wonderful, cigar-smoking character was its former owner, and he still holds court there every day at the cocktail hour. That day, as we waited for Ellis, Rudy regaled us with stories about the history of Gulf Hills—from its beginnings in 1927 as a Dude Ranch and hideaway for Al Capone and other mobsters, to the 1950s and '60s when Gulf Hills was a relaxing getaway for Elvis.

Ellis Branch arrived with his close friend, Maria Mavar, who added to the conversation. By the time Ellis got around to discussing the value of our house, we had heard about ocean voyages, the Walter Anderson Museum of Art, and several other equally marvelous subjects. Our meeting was as much a social occasion as it was a business meeting.

That's the way Mississippians conduct their business. As in Japan and South America, people sidle into business talks here. Business meetings are not cut and dried, but often freewheeling, pleasant encounters that lead to amicable deals. Although we never sold the house—we lost it shortly thereafter in Hurricane Katrina—I think of Ellis as more a friend than a business acquaintance, because our interactions were full of fun.

To a northerner, the ways of southerners can be mysterious, and southern politeness often seems hypocritical, to say nothing of a waste of time. One friend, an intelligent young Pennsylvanian, lived in Mississippi for three years and worked in Alabama. One day her boss, a native southerner, called her into the office and asked that she close the door. My friend took her seat with some apprehension. Her boss began the conversation, politely inquiring, "How's your mama?" and then proceeded languidly to other small talk, slowly working up to the purpose of the visit as tactfully and thoughtfully as possible. After listening to these pleasantries for about two minutes, my friend couldn't take another minute of her "tact." "All right! Cut the crap!" she demanded. "Why is the door closed?"

I find southern manners endearing. Because "four-letter ladies" aren't common in small town social life, men don't usually use coarse language in front of women. Jerry told me that his father used to say, "Southern men have two vocabularies, one for just men and another when women are present." Unfortunately, this tradition is fading. And what a pity! I hope any southern men reading this will immediately reinstate their former language in front of ladies.

I love that southern chivalry! Southern gentlemen do still open doors for women. They walk on the street side of the sidewalk, and they pull out the lady's chair when dining in a fine restaurant or at a dinner party. A few men even still order for their female companions, though this is anachronistic, even in Mississippi.

Good manners in Mississippi cut across all socio-economic backgrounds. Once, when I was buying a nightstand, the salesman called over a handyman. He was a muscular, fifty-year old man with a beard, a bandana, and an earring. He said he was an ex-marine and Vietnam vet. This didn't surprise me because, aside from his luminous eyes, there was nothing soft about him. But when I introduced myself with a casual, "Hi, I'm Daisy," he responded, "Charmed, I'm sure." No one, anywhere, has ever said such a thing to me! I've encountered that phrase only in classic films and nineteenth century novels.

Southern manners are perhaps best defined by what they're not. In New York, everyone has an opinion and seems compelled to express it. At a social occasion, however, southerners don't foist their opinions on others. Most of them keep their judgments to themselves, sensitive to the possibility that someone present might not share that point of view. What passes for intellectual discourse in the Northeast Corridor is often, I think, just an opportunity for confrontation. New Yorkers are determined and tough and they love to mix it up—all having to do with living in one of the most competitive cities in the world. New York even defeated the writer John Steinbeck after his first attempt to make a living there. "The city had beaten the pants off me," he said later. "Whatever it required to get ahead, I didn't have. I didn't leave the city in disgust—I left it with the respect plain unadulterated fear gives."

By comparison, living in Mississippi is easy. If any newcomers to Mississippi have been defeated by confrontation in recent years, I've never heard of it.

Southern manners don't reflect the southerner's lack of attention, but in fact, a large measure of close attention. In the anonymity of big city life (which I did love for its privacy), an individual may be easily forgotten or overlooked or disregarded. But in a small southern town, people aren't ignored. The people pay attention to each other. Awareness of one another is the norm. Mississippians connect. They place a higher value on people than on money and time.

This fact struck me recently when my husband and I were dining in a Biloxi restaurant, and I overheard a voluble, young pony-tailed waitress speaking to an elderly couple at the next table. The server was enthusiastically describing food, but the dishes she discussed weren't on our menu. After she walked away, the couple turned to us and explained that their waitress, whose husband was a chef, had just returned from Orlando, and she was relaying details about her vacation. "Just so you know what the conversation was about," they said. They didn't want us to feel excluded. There's a personal quality in this behavior—a thoughtfulness, a caring. In the Deep South, you see acts of inclusion like this everywhere—in the supermarket and the drugstore, at the dry cleaner and the gym.

A well-mannered southerner doesn't tell you how you should live your life. Southerners consider such presumption arrogance, and good manners require humility. This humility is one of the most attractive aspects of Mississippi character, a quality that lies at the heart of good manners.

Before the "Do Not Call" list made America's dinner hour more pleasant, I was struck by how patiently my husband listened to the entire speech a telemarketer gave. I asked Jerry why he listened to all that talk even though he knew he wasn't going to buy whatever the caller was selling. He explained, "That man isn't trying to bother me; he's just trying to make a living."

To me, Jerry's response epitomizes southern manners—acts of kindness, deeply and honestly felt. Good manners like these make existence with one's fellow human beings in Mississippi pleasurable.

No Complaints, No Confessions

MISSISSIPPI HAS HAD ITS SHARE of bad luck. This state has lost a staggering number of its young men in combat. Of the seventy-eight thousand Mississippi soldiers who fought in the Civil War, nearly thirty thousand died. Black Mississippians were enslaved; it would be more than a century before their lives were truly improved. In 1919, a boll weevil infestation destroyed this state's cotton industry, devastating an economy that was totally dependent upon agriculture. The Great Flood of 1927 overwhelmed the Mississippi Delta, causing a human death toll of one thousand people—the greatest natural disaster America had seen up to that point. The Candlestick Park tornado of 1966, the most ruinous and longest-tracked tornado that central Mississippi suffered in the twentieth century, caused fifty-eight deaths and more than five hundred injuries.

In 1969, Hurricane Camille claimed 131 lives on the Mississippi Coast, and another forty-one were missing; nearly ten thousand people were injured. Five thousand homes were completely destroyed, and forty thousand severely damaged. The storm laid waste the coastal cities of Waveland, Bay St. Louis, Pass Christian, Long Beach, Gulfport, Biloxi, Ocean Springs, and other smaller ones, entirely demolishing scores of businesses and severely damaging a greater number.

But Hurricane Katrina was worse. Katrina struck with a thirty-foot storm surge. The force of the hurricane destroyed more than seventy thousand homes. Our beautiful tree-lined coastal highway, U.S. Highway 90, was underwater for five hours. We have lost almost ninety percent of our shoreline trees; and huge, gaping spaces exist where buildings once stood and foliage grew. Ten churches in the Catholic diocese of Biloxi were either gutted or entirely wiped out. Of nine Episcopalian churches on the Mississippi Gulf Coast, Katrina took away six of them. All the other coastal churches were severely damaged or leveled. The Dantzler House, which served as the Mardi Gras Museum, is gone. It had just been remodeled. The Brielmaier House (circa 1895), an exquisite example of Victorian architecture, stood on the Town Green. It's gone. The Pleasant Reed House on the site of the Ohr-O'Keefe Museum is gone. So much history and beauty have vanished forever. Even the casinos' luck ran out; each took a terrible blow. The suffering of those who lost loved ones in this most calamitous of storms is staggering. I find no words to express the depth of such unhappiness.

This small state of Mississippi has seen a disproportionate amount of tragedy. But its inhabitants don't focus on their sorrows. They talk about "building back."

IN NINE YEARS of making south Mississippi my home, I've witnessed Mother Nature's cruelty as her ferocious winds pounded concrete houses into submission and her monsoon-like rains, driven by merciless gusts, felled trees that had been standing three hundred years and more. I've watched friends and neighbors lose ones they love to illness and old age; I've seen them endure in silent anguish when serious health problems afflicted multiple members of their families. Subject to all the tribulation that is humanity's lot, the southerner possesses a fierce pride and bears his trials quietly. You can make this observation of many communities worldwide, as stoicism in the face of adversity isn't connected to geography. However, in an America changed dramatically by the "let it all hang out" philosophy of the 1960s, and defined today by TV reality shows and the confessions of shameless celebrities, it's refreshing to live among those who maintain a sense of privacy.

Here, to be public about your troubles is to be ill-mannered. On my island of Manhattan, "kvetching" was standard practice. If you met a particularly complaining associate for cocktails in your favorite watering hole at the end of an arduous day, the standard response to the platitudinous "How are you?" was "Don't ask!" A recitation of grievances followed. The listener then tried to top that diatribe with "Ya shudda had my day!" We didn't take this ritual too seriously, but in a city of constant challenges and time pressure, we vented with gusto. The more you complained, it seemed, the more important your life was.

In West Hollywood, with its abundance of transplanted New Yorkers, people echoed this routine. Carping took on a different feel, but it was basic to the fabric of that golden world where everyone was seeking the conspicuously successful life. When the dream seeker realized that the fantasy was not within his easy reach, the grumbling began, although now the ingrate sported a tan. The venue had changed from the St. Regis to the Beverly Hills Hotel or from a corner coffee shop to the apartment courtyard swimming pool, but the attitude was the same. In the environs of the Hollywood Hills, if you were a beautiful young woman or man, you hoped someone important would hear your story and rescue you from your predicament or suggest a talent agent on Sunset Boulevard who was looking for just your dilemma to air on the newest episode. If life was a movie, you never knew—it could be you!

In the Deep South people wear their troubles gracefully. This hearkens back to a time in our country's history (not so long ago) when your life was your own business, and sharing personal information was what my husband calls, "self gossip."

Geographically isolated for most of its history, the South hasn't always kept up with the times. The inclination of southerners to hold on to familiar ways and old attitudes has sometimes led to undesirable consequences. But the same mindset has caused them to cling steadfastly to traditions of everlasting value, as well. The people of the South haven't turned their backs on the unwritten rules of politeness and courtesy passed down to them. They're not overly concerned with being "with it." Secure in the knowledge that such courtesies have survived because they're essential to making life bearable, southerners prevail through life's traumas with a gracious smile when asked how they are faring.

IN A SCENE from Damon Runyon's *Guys and Dolls*, Adelaide talks about psychology to her boyfriend, Nathan Detroit (Frank Sinatra in the movie version). He replies with "Naah, I don't got psychology," assuring her that he is not ill. Mississippians are kind of like that.

Surely Mississippians, like contemplative people the world over, ponder their inner life. I suppose they commune with themselves. Mississippians do not, however, get involved in lengthy discussions about "the meaning of the meaning." What a relief! I'm not suggesting that psychotherapy has not come to Mississippi, nor am I disparaging all forms of psychiatry. People in Mississippi have therapists as they do in other parts of the country, but they keep it quiet, as they are appropriately private. It's relaxing to be with people who talk about the weather, their jobs, their vacation, and a new restaurant rather than their tortured psyches. In this overpsychologized age we live in, the southerners I know don't examine every action. They allow themselves just to be. Introspection frequently gives way to narcissism, but that kind of self-obsession isn't a part of the southern mentality. Their hospitality, good manners, and lack of complaining all reflect the mental health of people native to these parts. If you're interested in other people and the world around you, your own little problems don't seem that important.

The airing of one's plight is so common in New York and L.A. that I daresay few, if any, people in those cities will agree with me. They don't even notice that, aside from discussing Seventh Avenue and "the Industry," they're always talking about themselves. New York has the largest number of psychiatrists in our country, followed by California. Live in the South for a number of years, though, and it becomes clear that Mississippians are more interested in you and all of your positive characteristics, than in the products of a troubled mind. Give to others, and your problems diminish. Explore your own psyche night and day, and you'll be a bore.

Southerners have a sounder approach to life, I think. They understand that convivial conversation is not about one's travails. It is an engagement with the greater world. I love knowing that when I go out for a social occasion I will not have to answer a barrage of personal questions or listen to the value of psychotherapy and a laundry list of complaints.

It's restful to be with southerners. And that's a big part of what makes living in Mississippi easy.

Southerners Talking

To BE SOUTHERN is to talk. Southerners seem to have a story for any topic that comes up. This quality fascinates me, since I've always been an avid listener. Eavesdropping on the dinner conversations at restaurants, in fact, was my greatest pleasure when traveling alone. Before I married Jerry, I always traveled singly. As a solo traveler not obligated to talk to a tablemate, I had the opportunity to listen in on diners chatting in many cities. The dialogue was fascinating, and it followed distinct patterns.

In Los Angeles, the chitchat is always about "the Industry"—everyone's an actor in L.A. In the Hamptons, the topic is real estate; in DC, politics; and in Chicago, people talk about sports. When the grand jury's indictment of "Scooter" Libby was announced, all three networks interrupted their regular programming, except in Chicago, where they aired the White Sox victory parade. In my former New York environs, the conversation is fashion. I've learned much more about upcoming trends by listening to conversations in restaurants on Seventh Avenue than I have by reading *Vogue*.

You can sit in almost any eating establishment in these major cities or be a guest in someone's home there, and before you've finished your appetizer, the particular regular topic of that locale will surface. Before I moved to the South, I thought the favorite subject of conversation would be the Civil War. And, yes, Civil War history still lives in the collective psyche, but not so much in the collective talk. I discovered very soon that the fondest conversation topics for southerners are family and food. No matter what else is going on in the world, those two topics pervade southern conversations and generate passionate dialogue.

People in the South discuss their families at length. I don't mean they talk incessantly about their children and the activities of their immediate households. They talk about their ancestors, people they may never have known.

Because few Mississippians ever move away from the state and comparatively few "outsiders" have moved into Mississippi, people here have numerous blood relatives—or, as they say, "kinfolks," or people they're "kin to." In this region there are families that have inhabited this area for two centuries—maybe even more. Mississippi families overlap and intertwine with each other; and this means that people are also connected closely to their in-laws and in-laws of in-laws.

Conversation centers on distant relatives, very distant relatives, and those to whom one is "undoubtedly" related. To keep track of all the cousins, once and twice removed, on the matrilineal line is not for the faint of heart. Yet for Mississippians, these names seem etched in memory. They can tell you stories that date back decades, if not centuries, all of them a cherished part of their oral history. Two Mississippians can spend an entire evening going through family names and oft-told stories trying to determine how they're related to each other. (They know they are related, because Great Aunt Susie said so.)

Unlike many parts of contemporary America, where people live in the moment and gaze towards the future, Mississippians live a life that is one long continuum, dating back to the earliest ancestors they know of. And they continue to value their native soil, no matter how far from it they have ventured.

A friend of ours, whose family has lived in Hattiesburg, Mississippi, for two hundred years, was shocked when I told him that our mutual friend, a mature woman who has lived in New Orleans for the last twenty years, had not returned to her home state of Mississippi to retire. "Isn't she going to come back?" he asked incredulously. "Her roots are in Mississippi."

JUST AS MISSISSIPPIANS love their families unconditionally (notwithstanding the occasional family feud), they also unreservedly love their food. Recipes are handed down lovingly from generation to generation.

It was late morning as Jerry and I drove out of New Orleans a week before our wedding. I had first seen Ocean Springs the previous week during a night out, but this was my first glimpse of Mississippi by daylight. The water was unusually blue that day, a perfect day to be initiated into the world of coastal Mississippi food. Jerry took me to lunch at Mary Mahoney's Old French House Restaurant. Where better to experience this significant rite of passage than surrounded by friendly jacketed waiters in an elegant French colonial landmark that has served fine coastal cuisine for decades? My meal that day, the first of many, was stuffed snapper—red snapper filled with shrimp and crabmeat in a rich cream sauce. I savored every divine morsel.

IN NEW YORK AND L.A.—especially L.A.—having lunch with a girlfriend is an agonizing, decision-making process. First, there's the lengthy study of the menu—Hollywood actor-waiters are inured. Then you select that food least damaging to your weight. At lunch in Beverly Hills, a colleague sent back a bottle of flavored water when she learned, after scrutinizing the label, that it had one calorie. In that golden land, where bars specialize in wheat grass juice, people actually fear food. If my friends or I weakened and indulged in dessert, we forgave ourselves only after we had gone to the gym and worked it off. People in the South seem to feel neither guilty nor apologetic for eating something they like—no matter how fattening! (After all, tomorrow is another day.)

In Mississippi, when I first broached the subject of some dishes containing too much fat (though tasty) or too many carbohydrates or too much sugar, Mississippians stared at me with an indulgent, half-pitying smile. When I overhear culinary conversations in Mississippi, I never hear about calories. I just hear comments like "Now, if you want your Mississippi Mud Pie to be really good, you have to add more . . . ."

The southerner's sheer joy of eating wends itself regularly into conversation. The merits of this or that food and the talents of one chef or another are carefully scrutinized. Mississippians speak tirelessly and lovingly of Robert St. John, a chef and food writer from Hattiesburg, as well as the triumvirate of New Orleans superstars—His Wit, Emeril Lagasse; Susan

Spicer, whose hippie look belies the elegance of her food; and His Theatricality, Paul Prudhomme, and his turducken. (For the uninitiated, a turducken is a deboned turkey stuffed with a deboned duck that's stuffed with a deboned chicken and seasoned generously with Cajun spices.) And, of course, the conversation includes the late great Craig Claiborne, *New York Times* food writer, whose love of good food stemmed from growing up in his mother's boarding house in Indianola, Mississippi. Home cooks deliberate about the quality and quantity of ingredients. Not only am I out of my depth in these food discussions, I am mystified.

Cannes and New York may have their film festivals, but the Mississippi Gulf Coast has food festivals: the Biloxi Seafood Festival, crawfish festivals, the Blessing of the Fleet, and the Shrimp Queen Pageant. There are crawfish cook-offs and an apparently endless number of other food contests. The beauty of

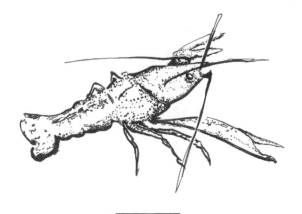

these food competitions is that there's no mean-spiritedness about them. After all, it's hard to be a sore loser when you're cheerfully consuming the winning recipes.

On the Mississippi Gulf Coast, food doesn't divide people; food unifies. There's the sheer fun of eating, of course. At the 2006 Coliseum Crawfish Festival, festival-goers consumed fifteen thousand pounds of crawfish—seven-and-a-half tons—and that's a lot of crawfish! But Mississippi Gulf Coast food festivals are about much more than food; they're about connecting people—linking the generations and bringing together diverse social, economic, and ethnic groups. Food is an excuse for Mississippians to get together and talk.

You're Not from Here, Are You?

"**I**S THAT TIGHT ENOUGH?**" She eyed me critically. Deanna Adriano was inserting safety pins in the waist of my slacks, as I stood on the wooden box facing the mirror. Fully concentrating, she appraised the lines of the pantsuit, checking to see that it looked perfect. This was my first dealing with this dressmaker, and I was impressed with her professionalism. Deanna is from Brazil, and we were speaking German.

A COMMON MISCONCEPTION about Mississippi is that the inhabitants are all WASPs, most of them Bubbas. Delightfully, Mississippi provides more variety than I had imagined. Although most Mississippians are, in fact, Protestants with ancestry in the British Isles—or Africa—the state's population includes descendents from every continent. The Mississippi River towns—Natchez, Vicksburg, and

Greenville—the Delta, and Jackson all have diverse populations that date from the nineteenth century. Jews have lived in Mississippi since the early 1800s, immigrating first from Germany and later from eastern Europe. Slaves cleared the Delta wilderness; Catholic Italians, Chinese, and eastern European Jews established its early businesses. Greek and Lebanese families are prominent in the state's past and present. Native Mississippians, the Choctaw Indians, have a thriving community in Neshoba County. Their own casinos have made them prosperous, yet they continue to celebrate many of their traditional arts and customs.

The Gulf Coast is the most ethnically diverse section of Mississippi. Originally a French colony, the Coast honors its Catholic French heritage in Mardi Gras celebrations. Eastern European settlers have been an intrinsic part of coastal Mississippi since the late 1800s. Largely Catholic, they're embedded in south Mississippi's history. The budding Gulf Coast seafood industry at the turn of the twentieth century attracted many Slovenian immigrants and Louisiana Cajun migrants, among others. Catholic Italians developed the seafood trade and international shipping business. In 1932, C.F. Gollot began selling fresh seafood out of the back of his refrigerated truck in Hattiesburg, Tupelo, Meridian, and other land-locked Mississippi towns without access to fresh seafood. So the Biloxi seafood industry has informed the tastes of other Mississippians.

The Slovenians placed a special stamp on the culture of the Coast by introducing the annual celebration, the Blessing of the Fleet, one of the high points of the year. Year 2007 marks the seventy-ninth annual Biloxi Blessing of the Fleet. In this ritual, a priest sprinkles holy water on each of the shrimp boats and other vessels going out to sea at the start of the new season and gives his blessings for safe passage and a successful catch. The ceremony culminates by releasing an evergreen wreath into the Biloxi channel to commemorate the fishermen who have been lost at sea. One of the most beloved customs in the larger coastal community, the Blessing of the Fleet reinvigorates the Biloxi seafood industry annually and unifies the coastal community. The Slovenian heritage of many of Biloxi's residents is also reflected in their love of the sea and in their skill as fishermen.

There are about ten thousand Vietnamese living in south Mississippi. Newly arrived as refugees in the 1970s, they have integrated themselves into the larger coastal lifestyle, while maintaining their identities. Most of them are Roman Catholic, and most of the others are Buddhists. Family oriented and industrious, most Vietnamese earn their living as fishermen. The presence of Vietnamese people on the Mississippi Gulf Coast adds immeasurably to the international feel, enhancing it with Vietnamese restaurants, groceries, and music. Sadly, Hurricane Katrina caused many hardships and severely affected their livelihoods.

By early 2007, the fresh shrimp and oysters were mostly back, but the absence of infrastructure had kept many shrimpers onshore. With so many shattered restaurants, large wholesalers lost customers, and the demand for shrimp declined. Katrina also smashed or severely injured shrimp boats, shrimp processing structures, and storage buildings. A number of Vietnamese lived on their shrimp boats. When the storm demolished their boats, these fishermen lost their homes as well as their livelihood.

Since Hurricane Katrina, the Coast has received a large influx of Mexican workers. It will be interesting to see how well they adapt, with immigration now such a controversial national political issue. My fourteen years in Southern California—and several trips to Mexico—taught me that Mexicans are industrious people who love their children to distraction and practice a fervent, heart-felt Catholicism. In their deep Christian beliefs and dedication to family, they have a lot in common with Mississippians. Not to mention that they like their food spicy! If Mississippi history is any indication, the Mexican people and their traditions will become part of the cultural fabric of the Coast.

WHEN I DISCOVERED Phoenicia, owned and operated by Sam Sabbagh, a cordial Lebanese man, I knew I had found a treasure—authentic Mediterranean food. Although Hurricane Katrina caused massive damage, Phoenicia reopened after months of extensive repair, and it's better than ever. I always look forward to walking through the door, being warmly greeted by Sam, and sitting down to the most appetizing hummus, tasty rice, flavorful baba ganoush, and satisfying dolmas to be found anywhere.

Yearning for authentic Italian food in south Mississippi, I was thrilled when Pasta Italia opened its doors in the small town of D'Iberville, named for Pierre Le Moyne d'Iberville, the founder of the Louisiana colony. Michele D'Oto, the fabulous and agreeable chef and owner of Pasta Italia, is from Modena, and brought the pleasing dishes of his native northern Italy to his establishment here. Never have I tasted better lobster ravioli. Sadly, his cozy little eating-house, to which we used to bring our own wine, was decimated by the hurricane. He brought a bit of authentic Italy with him, and we miss him and his bistro. We also miss his charming European habit of kissing a lady's hand.

SINCE THE MISSISSIPPI GULF COAST is a busy international port, people of many nations are arriving continually, contributing to the energetic mix of people on the Coast. The strong presence of widely traveled military personnel at Keesler Air Force Base also enhances the international feel of the Coast. (My aerobics teacher, Carmen, from Chile, is married to a man stationed at Keesler.) The Stennis Space Center, NASA's primary testing facility, has brought to south Mississippi many highly educated scientists from other parts of this country and foreign countries, as well.

For more than one hundred years, the Mississippi Gulf Coast has been a winter haven for northeasterners and a place where many choose to retire. Generations of Louisiana and Mississippi families have spent their summer vacations here. In recent years, gambling casinos have lured increasing numbers of tourists the year-round. These things, together with the varied traditions brought by early immigrants, have made the Gulf Coast a place of tolerant, welcoming people.

We Got Time

I GROANED WHEN I SAW THE CARS backed up over Lake Pontchartrain. The drive from Ocean Springs to New Orleans usually takes one-and-a-half to two hours, depending upon the traffic. It's a ride I've always enjoyed, an easy trip. My favorite segment of it was the long bridge over Lake Pontchartrain, the huge, glassy lake that seemed to take forever to cross. On this fine day, I was on my way to a doctor appointment, and running late. Finally arriving, I rushed through the door and apologized to Pat, the affable, petite blonde bookkeeper who has worked for Dr. John Yarborough for a dozen years. "I'm sorry I'm late."

"You cain't be late in N'Awlins," she replied. And she was serious. No slightly annoyed tone, no condescending look, just a simple recognition that things happen, people run late, traffic jams occur. Since it's impossible to assure that you'll be on time, it's impossible to be late. After all, this is the Big Easy, the City that Care Forgot.

How surprised I was when, fresh from New York, I learned that Dr. Yarborough closed his office at lunch. This renowned dermatologist and his staff actually ate lunch during the lunch hour! I'd never heard of such a thing in New York and L.A. In truth, I found this quaint practice rather distressing—until I thought about it. It's really a much more humane approach to life. If Dr. Yarborough himself is an accurate gauge, taking time for lunch is an excellent prescription for a well-lived life.

No matter how busy Dr. Yarborough is, he always looks relaxed, and he takes time to chat in a genuinely friendly manner. He personifies the southern gentleman. A big man who wears beautiful suits and ties, he has compassionate eyes, a musical voice, and exquisite manners—and he's also an accomplished classical pianist and organist. John M. Yarborough, a native of a tiny Mississippi town (Pickens—population 1,200), has been a mainstay of the New Orleans community for decades. He has patiently taught residents at Tulane University's School of Medicine and serves actively on numerous boards and committees that actually get things done. Yet he never appears to be rushed.

On the drive back from New Orleans, between Slidell, Louisiana, and Ocean Springs on I-10, I invariably pass construction work along the interstate. I used to speed right by it, but I slow down now and appreciate the landscape. The overturned sand is a blazing orange-red. (So that's what the "red earth of Tara" was about.) What a pity to speed through this stretch, missing mile after mile of brick-red soil, brilliant against the verdant countryside.

While time is relative and varies with cultures, to most Americans "time is money." It's different down South. The pace is slower. New Yorkers walk—almost jog—through the city; southerners stroll. Small shop owners here close their businesses whenever it suits them, without a worry about the commercial opportunities they miss. My friend, an exasperated northeasterner who lived in Mississippi for three years, said, "I don't understand these people. Doesn't anyone want to make money?" Of course, Mississippians do want to make money enough to live, but they emphasize living over making money. They prefer a rhythm that makes living easier, more pleasant, and more relaxed, instead of the inhuman pace dictated by the digital world.

A fast moving, fast talking person, I was in my element in New York's tempo. Everything seemed urgent. Time was something I worked against. Everybody did. I was constantly checking my watch to make sure I could finish one activity and get on the next one in time and on time. Racing against time is a way of life, and I didn't know any other way.

But in the Deep South, I've learned how much more pleasurable it is to savor time than to compete with it. My husband (who doesn't like to be rushed) makes a distinction between what appears to be urgent and what is truly important. I've come to appreciate the wisdom of his distinction. Things at work seemed to need my urgent attention. But were they important?

THE FRONT PORCH symbolizes an approach to life that's unhurried and sweet, calling to mind Bertrand Russell's observation: "Time you enjoyed wasting is not wasted time."

I can't imagine the South without its front porches. Houses in the Deep South have always featured front porches. In the days before air conditioning or even electric fans, large porches were essential for survival in the South, providing places for people to escape the scorching sun or the heat trapped inside stuffy homes. Some homes also had back porches and side porches, but in old houses, the front porch was always the largest and most important. The front porch brought the community right to one's doorsteps. It was a place for socializing, for meeting and greeting people and sharing news and gossip. Today porches aren't as necessary for escaping the heat, but they're still important for creating and maintaining a sense of community.

In south Mississippi, middle class suburbanites

gather on their front porches, something that's less likely to happen in northern states. There, social activity occurs in the backyard, away from prying eyes. Front porches and front yards, too, are about openness; they welcome people. Elderly people, who aren't as mobile as they once were, can still connect to the outside world by sitting on their porch.

When we were newly married, I suggested to Jerry that we fence off our property. He hesitated and then said, "It would look unfriendly." This concept—that we might appear unfriendly—had never occurred to me.

These beautiful outdoor rooms—in most cases, screened—seem meant for indolence and watching the world go by. In small towns you're not watching life's great pageant, but you will see your neighbors passing. And you'll enjoy the lazy afternoons and the greetings, especially when it's just too hot to move. With air conditioning, the habits of its occupants have changed somewhat, but, archaic or not, the southern porch still symbolizes an approach to life that's leisurely and gracious.

The front porch is a place to see and be seen. Those things take time. Tommy Neely is an extraordinary carpenter from Pascagoula and a southerner to his bones, and I've enjoyed many conversations with him. He took a trip to New York years ago. He didn't like it.

"What, in particular, displeased you?" I asked.

Laconic, lanky Tom replied, "People don't talk to you. Ah lahk sittin' on my porch and greetin' the neighbors."

It was a telling moment for me. With all of the things he might have complained about—Manhattan's noise, too many people, the pollution—he singled out the lack of time to exchange pleasantries with people. In New York, he couldn't make that connection with others that's so vital to Mississippians.

Recently, I read an article in *USA Today* about the resurgence of front porches in America. An increasingly alienated society, it seems, is rediscovering the appeal of a sun or sleeping porch. As far as the amiability of the porch is concerned, southerners are far ahead of most of the country. They have never given up this cherished tradition. They know a good thing when they see it.

I WAS STANDING in a supermarket checkout line one recent afternoon, and I noticed that there was no divider available to place between my groceries and those of the couple behind me. I offered either to make room for their purchases, or to let them go ahead of me. The gentleman gave me a relaxed smile and said, "It don't matter. We got time. Tomorrow ain't got here yet."

Domestic Arts

THE WATER WAS TRUE BLUE on this day. The Mississippi Gulf waters don't have that showy, aquamarine hue that you find in the Caribbean or Florida. The colors here are more discreet, playing in a minor key of blue-grey-pearl. The light softens everything, and because of this impressionistic haze, it's possible to overlook the delicate beauty of south Mississippi. But this was a particularly vivid day, and as I was driving down Highway 90, I opened my windows and breathed the freshness of the morning air. The cries of seagulls—that strange crescendo of "kaw kaw kaw kaw KAAAW" and then the fade-out—accompanied me on my journey. I thought about how the soft air and the water's movement help to create coastal Mississippi's distinctive moods, mellowing people's temperaments. I was looking forward to my first guild meeting.

I walked up the flagstone path that led to the home in Pass Christian (pronounced Christianne, with the emphasis on the last syllable). A tangerine-colored kitten was sunning himself on the lawn. Just ahead of me was a slim, white-haired woman who carried herself beautifully. I introduced myself as a new member, and she smiled gently and said, "Well, we are just delahted to have you!" I was glad that my premiere meeting was taking place in this graceful small town, popular with both the yachting set and antique lovers.

The Symphony Guild is the volunteer organization that supports the Gulf Coast Symphony Orchestra. Made up of more than one hundred women who meet monthly in members' homes, the guild has among its membership some of the most spirited women of Mississippi. On this day, members were arriving from all corners of the twenty-six-mile-long Mississippi Gulf Coast region, greeting each other animatedly, chatting about the most recent performance, and drinking sweetened tea. In this beautiful home I shut out the clamor of the rock-and-roll world we often find ourselves in today and relaxed in that ambiance of sensitivity and civility that mark the classical music lover.

Because the purpose of the Symphony Guild is to garner as much support as possible for the orchestra and to inform members of recent expenses and other business matters, I expected to receive practical information, coffee, and a few doughnuts. The meeting, however, greatly exceeded my expectations, which often has happened since I've lived in Mississippi.

We strolled into the house, and I was stunned. Here was sprawling Old World elegance. The luxury evoked the genteel plantation house of my imagination. Because "The Pass," as Pass Christian is locally known, is a historic neighborhood, I expected faded grandeur. But the hardwood floors gleamed, and the staircase was *Gone with the Wind*-worthy. Comfortable looking chairs and sofas in shades of ivory and white flanked the fireplace. The gorgeous wrought-iron fire screen was obviously handmade.

The dining room table, displaying a musical theme, truly enchanted me. I was a child again, looking at New York's Fifth Avenue windows at Christmas. Centrally placed was a little bust of Mozart. Antique parchment music paper, inscribed with the first few measures of a symphony, rested on a miniature music stand. Surrounding this old-fashioned arrangement was an array of aromatic dishes beautifully presented. I gazed at the inviting table. The abundance was overwhelming.

AS YOU'D EXPECT in a region of the country known for its hospitality, I've been invited to many homes. I've spent congenial evenings in unconventional houses and condos in New Orleans where the Mardi

Gras colors of purple, green, and gold are proudly and permanently on display, regardless of the season; sunny afternoons on the lawns of white-pillared Colonial Revival homes on the Mississippi Gulf Coast; and weekends on horse "farms" in Oxford, Mississippi. I've been a guest in a Corinth, Mississippi, home that's a jubilant expression of Margaritaville, right down to the palm trees; enjoyed dinner in Nashville backyards shaded by old, graceful trees; and after the loss of our hurricane-stricken home, received shelter in an oasis of calm in Fairhope, Alabama, surrounded by hanging flower baskets. And I have been repeatedly struck by this fact: all the homes are gorgeous! Their exquisite design and use of color has astonished me.

And the women usually decorate their own homes. Mississippians are especially house-proud. Their habitats are a form of self-expression—works of art. Even if their domains bear the stamp of the Old South, furnished with period pieces (it's not uncommon to have a great-great grandparent's rocking chair), each one reveals an individual touch.

In most places I've lived, an elegantly designed home usually expresses good, conservative taste. But in the Deep South, it also conveys a sense of fun. Sitting in the living room in Fairhope, I noticed a brass sign above the door that directed me "To the Lifeboats." My friend Anne decorated her son's condo in New Orleans, making his bathroom a sleek, urbane space. But when I looked at my reflection in the mirror, I laughed heartily at the little figurines of men dancing upside down on its surface. She had placed decals on the mirror so artfully that little men seemed to be looking under my skirt! Another New Orleanian has decorated her condo in a refined style, but her bathroom signs, written in French, are quite naughty.

I was surprised during an antique hunt with three Mississippi friends, when one of them purchased an object that looked as if it had come from a junkyard. This was beyond "distressed" furniture: it was the worst looking peeling chest of drawers I'd ever set eyes upon. I couldn't imagine it fitting in her 1970s modern house with its clean, contemporary lines and large glass windows. I assumed she had bought the chest because it was a bargain and planned to refinish it. To my amazement, her keen eye turned this dubious object into the perfect component for the corner of the dining room, which opens onto a charming country garden furnished with simple, handmade furniture. This rustic chest added warmth and created a harmonious flow between inside and out, transforming an empty space into one of character.

Lavish or simple, the southern woman's home is an expression of her personality. In it she places the best part of herself; adorns it with objects and photographs that connect her to the past, and creates nooks that invite engrossing conversation. Lighting is forgiving. Fabrics are cushy. After being offered a chair and a cocktail, I'm convinced that getting up again is an utter waste of time. As beautiful as these finely furnished houses are, they're not forbidding, but meant to be lived in. They all exude warmth and coziness. No areas are off-limits except to the occasional hyper-energetic pet.

One Christmas, I admired the striking cloth napkins at our friend Regan's home. "Oh," she said, "I sewed them just this morning." In Mississippi, almost every woman is a Martha Stewart. Southern women still practice "the domestic arts." But don't for a moment think that southern women are plain and practical. They talk about "tabletops" a lot. They're intimately familiar with Lenox china patterns, as my friend Lucy demonstrated one evening when she perused my table setting. "Oh, Autumn!" she exclaimed. "Arts" is the emphatic word in "domestic arts." Southern women can take the most pedestrian function and transform it into an aesthetic experience.

IN MY FORMER metropolitan life, I spent hours in the residences of friends, lingering over coffee and brandy, savoring the cool, modern ambiance. I've lived high up above it all—on the thirty-sixth floor in Tribeca, overlooking the Hudson, magical at night.

In New York, and in L.A., creative men and women embellish their homes stylishly, but only a handful are memorable. In Mississippi, a stunning, gracefully appointed house is not the exception, but the rule.

New Yorkers spend most of their time away from their homes. City life offers such a multitude of diversions that one's residence doesn't have to be the center of social activities. Since apartments are frequently small, entertaining in restaurants is the most common and pleasant way to get together with friends or family. In small southern towns, you have to create more of your own pleasures, so home is a vital, vibrant center of life.

Good Friends and Friendly People

"**W**ILL YOU BREAK BREAD with me?" a smiling Will Denton asked as he offered a basket of warm, fragrant rolls. Jerry had just introduced me to the slight bearded man and his self-possessed wife Lucy over dinner at an Ocean Springs restaurant. His Biblical turn of phrase fascinated me: there was such grace in it.

Will was a prominent Mississippi attorney with a brilliant career. He was a decorated Vietnam War veteran, a powerful advocate of those less fortunate, and a community leader with a strong sense of civic responsibility. To me, Will Denton, embodied Longfellow's words, "Hospitality sitting with gladness."

I picture Will, a man with a dry sense of humor and a poker-faced delivery, only the faintest light in his eye, hinting that he was going to spin a yarn. He was fun, a host who enjoyed life. Like his intelligent, porcelain-skinned Lucy, he enjoyed his parties as much as his guests did. He served me venison once, but, unsure of my dietary habits, told me it was turkey. He convinced me that cutting up masses of huge scallions grown in his garden was an annual event, and he invited me to help with the slicing. I had already learned that Mississippians would use any excuse to have a party, so I didn't doubt him. Maybe it was Green Onion Day or some odd state custom.

Will Denton has gone to his heavenly reward. He acted as an informal legal advisor to his friend, John Grisham, who delivered the eulogy. Avid hunter that Will was, the turkeys and deer in Brooklyn, Mississippi, are resting easy now. He exemplified the gladness of southern hospitality, and his welcoming cheer remains with me.

While all America is rightly known for its generous spirit, southern hospitality enjoys a particular cachet. Recognized for gracious living on wicker-stuffed porches, barbeques with raucous laughter, and celebrations that seem to go on forever, the South has earned its reputation for high-quality entertainment.

But southern hospitality goes deeper than mere amusement. I refer to friendliness that's heart-felt. The southern hospitality that I've experienced is an expression of the goodness of the people here.

In a 1971 interview with a regular participant at the weeklong, live-in Neshoba County Fair, Mrs.

Arwin Deweese Turner conveys the joyous spirit of Mississippians. When interviewer Charlotte Capers marveled at the bountiful spread in Mrs. Turner's cabin, the hostess explained,

We do hope that everybody will feel welcome to come. We don't particularly have to know the people, just so they come and enjoy the day. We love to feed them and refresh them and have them with us.

"POKE THEM LIPS OUT, BOY," the huge man said, his voice booming. He wore overalls, a fire-engine red baseball cap, and a bright red T-shirt, and his beard was a milder shade of red. "Mommy will always be stronger than you, no matter how strong you think you are."

Looking up at this "giant" was a two-year-old-boy, who was pouting because his mother wouldn't let him have the run of the medical center waiting room. I was the amused observer as I waited for my husband who was having his annual physical.

While the boy moped through his terrible two's, his mom and the large man, strangers to one another, began a conversation. The reception room was crowded and becoming more so. The giant remarked at how quickly it was filling up. A middle-aged woman, watching the little boy and the adult conversation, joined in. She pointed out a couple of others in the throng. "Those are third and fourth cousins over there. They're much younger than I am." Now there was a three-way conversation going on. "My brother lives in Wal-Mart," a youngish woman remarked to the stranger in the next seat. Babies and children were everywhere. Cell phones were ringing all over the place, and no two-ring tones were alike. Two muscular men in jeans and work boots, probably Mexican, were conversing softly in Spanish.

Reading matter was scattered on tables and magazine racks, but no one was reading. Everyone preferred to speak with the nearest person. A very young woman sitting next to her grandmother held in her arms a brand new baby boy swathed in blue. He was hiccupping, tiny infant hiccups. We all smiled. A tall blonde in an advanced state of pregnancy checked in at the reception desk, explaining that the little boy with her, a cherubic-looking five-year-old, had a Q-tip stuck in his ear. She sat down wearily but calmly, and the stranger next to her asked what had happened. The expecting lady recounted how her daughter Jennifer shrieked when she discovered her younger brother's ear dilemma.

"Come here, Boy. Don't you run away from me," a thirty-something father commanded of his blonde eighteen-month-old son. To my northern ear, "boy" always sounds vaguely threatening, but the father gently placed his son on his lap and kissed his forehead. The baby had a flyer that he couldn't read, and his dad was looking at a Spanish One review book, but obviously unable to concentrate. The drama of life going on in the lobby drew his attention. His eyes wandered to a youthful mother with her girlfriend or sister and a baby about four months old. She was speaking loudly into her cell phone, "Ah'm not holdin' him down while he gets his shot. You have to come over here."

In Mississippi, there are no strangers—only unmet friends.

The next day, I was again in a doctor's waiting room, this one in New Orleans. New Orleans is a fantastic city, and I love it. I love New Orleanians for their spicy individuality, but they are just not as approachable as Mississippians. In this waiting room, people glanced up from magazines when a new patient walked in, then immediately returned their eyes to the page, just as they do in New York. Everyone seemed polite, but not free and easy enough to be friendly, the way Mississippians are.

No one would ever mistake the doctor's receiving room in New Orleans for anything else. A person walking into the medical receiving room in Biloxi, however, might have mistaken it for a party.

The Southern Lady: Alive and Well

I EXPECTANTLY OPENED the cheerful invitation. Its brightness matched the early summer day. Our yard had come alive with white and pink crape myrtles; the Japanese magnolia tree had finally blossomed; and the oleanders were out in full bloom. Across the bayou, the noise of our neighbor's motorboat was receding, now just a hum as it made its way to distant waters. Abbie, the Aussie German shepherd that lived next door, bounded about, unsuccessfully chasing a squirrel as if it were a mortal enemy.

The invitation from my friend Lucy requested the pleasure of my company at an afternoon party introducing her son Walt's fiancée to the circle of female friends and acquaintances who would soon become part of her life and embrace her with southern sisterhood. Such an occasion isn't an engagement shower—no gifts are involved—but, in fact, it has elements of a debutante's tea, with the newly affianced woman standing in a receiving line with her future mother-in-law. It's a gracious way of welcoming the newcomer—one of many social graces that distinguish the lives of Mississippi women. In the Denton's magnificent white-columned house on the day of the party, I thought about how fine it would be if we welcomed newcomers this way north of the Mason-Dixon line.

Southern ladies still practice other rituals that are disappearing elsewhere in the United States. They send handwritten thank-you notes, no matter how simple a dinner they've enjoyed. Although they have as much Internet access as anyone anywhere, they don't use e-mail to express gratitude or sympathy. They take the time to stamp an elegant envelope—beautiful stationery is customary—and mail it. They take pride in nice penmanship, and a letter from a southern lady usually has the perfect look of what we used to call in New York "parochial school handwriting"—legible, even, never a scrawl. And the southern woman always mentions something specific that she particularly enjoyed about an evening spent in your company. There's nothing generic about her note. It is for you, and only you.

The beauty and grace of the south Mississippi I love—the heirloom silver, the carefully tended gardens, the elegant cocktail parties, the pearls, and the antique furniture—would not be here without the southern lady. Without her the Gulf Coast, while naturally blessed, would be little more than a place to go fishing and hunting. The southern lady doesn't need expensive silver and priceless antiques, however, to work her magic.

Never has this been more apparent than after Hurricane Katrina destroyed so many of these luxuries. It was Thanksgiving 2005—less than three months after the storm. Jerry and I were temporarily living in Fairhope, and our friends Lucy, Claire, and DeLo, who had all lost their homes as well, were now living together in a tiny fixer-upper in Biloxi. It was still the worst of times for most of us, but we decided to celebrate Thanksgiving together, grateful to be alive. We had shrimp cocktails and drinks on the tiny porch, which was unscreened and faced a dismal-looking street. Because the oven didn't work, Lucy and friends prepared the entrée in the kitchen, but Courtney had to keep driving back and forth to her home to pop things into the oven.

It was a far cry from the gracious living of better times. But like Scarlett O'Hara and the famous drapes, these southern ladies used the resources they had. They placed a bowl of lemons as a centerpiece on the coffee table in the cramped living room. Fresh flowers adorned the table in the minuscule dining room, and glowing candles surrounded us as we gathered at the table to say grace. I don't know how all eleven of us plus a five-month-old baby managed to fit into that dining room, but it was inviting and lovely, and we were happy to be there. Creating this scene had nothing to do with money; it had everything to do with these women's appreciation of beauty and friendship—and their good taste, which, once cultivated, is not easily lost.

SOUTHERN WOMEN know to exercise restraint when making a new acquaintance. Mastering the art of enjoyable small talk must be something ladies in Mississippi learn early. They don't try to put you on the spot. In the northern cities, I know many women, even those who appear quite polished, who immediately begin aggressively questioning a person they've just met. Whether this practice has always been the case, I don't know, but I've noticed it frequently over the last twenty years.

Women of Mississippi possess a ladylike reserve, especially when meeting men. By "ladylike reserve" I don't mean submissiveness: many confident women, who hold their own with men in business dealings and intellectual pursuits, practice lady-like reserve. I mean that women here don't seem to have to be visible all the time. There's often a softness or gentleness in their speech. They can be assertive, but they're rarely aggressive. Though southern men don't seem comfortable with aggressive women, I've found them perfectly relaxed with confident women. The southern woman's self-assured reserve is something her northern sisters ought to emulate. It puts strangers at ease.

Oh, and southern women don't curse…or, as they say, "cuss."

SITTING AT THE NEXT TABLE in the King Cole room of the St. Regis Hotel in New York, the expensive-looking blonde perched prettily on her chair. She was speaking with a man she had just met. I watched her, as, not five minutes into the conversation, chin resting on her young hand, she began her interrogation. "So, are you married?" she queried, leaning towards her prey. She followed with a succession of inquiries about his personal and professional life: "Why did you get a divorce? Do you have kids? Do your children live with you or with their mother? How long have you been with that company? Do you plan to stay?" On and on, the staccato interrogation continued, disrupting the flow of any real conversation they might have had. Although he politely answered her questions (he was single and worked in advertising), he was obviously uncomfortable with the directness and haste of her approach. A potentially romantic evening was quickly losing its promise.

I think about New Yorkers and compare them to the people who live in Mississippi. New York is full of attractive, stylish, smart, and hardworking women. Manhattan's vitality draws upon the world's most gifted and ambitious people, arriving in droves with new résumés and fresh faces, starry-eyed and ready to prove themselves. I've shared humor and heartbreak with them. And while New York women enthusiastically pursue careers to which they're committed, deep in their hearts they're also looking for Prince Charming. Many of them are embarrassed to admit it, but it's clear over cocktail conversation that the intoxication of the pulse-quickening atmosphere of professional life in the city is just not enough. And it's their longing for romance that causes many women to falter. They don't seem to understand that you cannot go after a man the way you pursue a new client or new account—that in fact, you don't go after a man at all. They could use the help of their southern sisters.

In the dance of romance, southern women more closely resemble their European counterparts. They don't approach a man "head-on." Given a scenario like the one above, Mississippi women wouldn't ask those questions. A Mississippi belle allows the man to wonder if she's married and lets him struggle as he tries to assess the situation. This is not manipulation; it's diplomacy.

Nor do women of the Deep South immediately ask a man what he does for a living. They're well aware that men, who define themselves so much by their profession, will eventually tell them. They banter; they flirt; and they know when to be silent. Unlike many northern women, women in the South are reticent about revealing their personal life to strangers. A Mississippi belle recognizes the importance of time and place. She appreciates the charm of a little old-fashioned behavior. And she remains enigmatic upon meeting a new man.

Be assured: the southern belle has not disappeared. She, as much as anyone, has helped Mississippi retain a sense of place.

MERRILL'S BLUE EYES were earnest as she cautioned me, "Let me give you some advice about bein' a southern belle. Mah mama told me that if you learn to do somethin', that becomes yo' job. If you learn how to make really great barbeque, you'll be standin' over that hot grill each tahm you decide to have a cook-out, so don't learn it unless you really want to do it, because it becomes yo' job." Newly married and brand new to the Mississippi Gulf Coast, I was amused. But now I see the wisdom of her counsel.

A key difference between southern and non-southern women is their relationship to work. Bright, educated, well-read, chic Mississippians, like women all over the States today, are teachers, doctors, marketing directors, lawyers, sales people, accountants, nurses, aerobics instructors, hair stylists, architects, television announcers, and valuable members of many other professions. They're ambitious and eager to use their degrees and capabilities and enjoy their careers. I've worked for them and with them; they possess an awareness that reaches far beyond the boundaries of Mississippi or its neighboring states. The "Information Age" has not passed them by.

In personal conversation, however, when these women talk about their potential, it's not limited to their academic and professional worth. They're skeptical of the idea that you "can have it all." Committed as they are to their families of origin, they're also devoted to friends, husbands, and children, and I haven't met one female here who felt that career success was more important or prestigious than individual happiness. Those who work outside the home are respected for their accomplishments but not more so than those who exercise their energies in the domestic realm.

The women I've met in Mississippi, whose friendships I value, don't appear to be tense and exhausted. They seem naturally to understand that hyperactivity creates frazzled people. They don't pull out their Palm Pilots and complain about their busy schedules, as many in the North tend to do. Yet anyone who observes their activities with the chamber of commerce, museum boards, and church and community organizations of every stripe, and knows how much time they spend chauffeuring children to school and after-school activities, can see that they're very busy and fulfilled. Women in Mississippi may expend as much energy on a church activity as they do in a corporate job. Perhaps more.

As women in the large urban areas struggle with the questions of whether to marry, have children, go to grad school while pursuing a career, or relocate some distance away for a job promotion, women here seem to prioritize with ease. Family comes first to a southern woman; she can pursue an occupation later. Even if she takes a job out of economic necessity or personal fulfillment, she puts her higher priority on family. No matter how interesting the work, it can be duplicated; loved ones cannot. And southern women don't lose sight of that. Just as Mississippi women aren't embarrassed about being religious, they're not ashamed to admit that love and marriage and family are at the top of the priority list. And this attitude prevails, whether the woman works outside the home or not, now or later.

My friend Vangie, a belle from Louisiana who devoted herself to being a wonderful wife and mother and a brilliant homemaker, decided at the age of forty that she wanted a job outside her home. She worked in a school for three years "and grew and grew and grew," she told me. Nonetheless, she missed being at home with her family, cooking gourmet meals (she has four stoves!), and attending to her elegant house and garden. She was at peace when she resigned.

Big-city life with its nonstop activity, excitement, and temptations is exhilarating. But along with this stimulating environment comes the social pressure to work—always work—no matter what. Cities like New York are filled with fascinating, high-energy career women, many with families, who are frazzled and struggle constantly to maintain their equilibrium. I just do not see such women in the South, whether they work outside the home or not. I think that southern women have actually found what most modern women are looking for, and that is balance.

Little Known Assets

YOU HAVE TO KNOW three things about southern men: They adore their mamas and call them
"Mama" long past childhood; they love football
almost as much as they love their mamas; and they
have the most glorious speaking voices anywhere.
I'm not referring to the appealing, famous drawl.
I'm speaking of a vocal tone—timbre and pitch—that
is exceptionally beautiful. At first, I thought only
my husband's voice was so silky. And it is—full of
warmth and understatement, accurate mirrors of his
character. But in time I detected this musical sound
among men throughout the state.

U.S. District Judge L.T. Senter Jr. also springs to
mind when I think of the musicality and cadence of
a southern man's voice. A dignified man appointed
to the bench by President Carter, Judge Senter has
"the wisest eyes you've ever seen," as my husband so

accurately observed. Judge Senter's voice carries a history that goes beyond his personal one. It's the voice of a man with roots deep in southern soil, and his calm, measured phrases give full expression to the collective experience of his fellow Mississippians. He has heard and judged many a story. When we walk away from an evening spent in his company, his rich voice stays with me.

I'm struck even more by the distinctive southern male voice when I travel outside the South. Wherever my journeys lead, I'm frequently jolted by the nasality, the whiny raspy quality present in men's speech. Returning to the soothing tones of southern men—sounds lacking aggression and pomp—always reassures me. Who hasn't been mesmerized by Shelby Foote's voice in the television documentary series, *The Civil War*?

If I ever again live outside the Deep South, the southern man's voice will be one of my most treasured memories. Like Marcel Proust's madeleine inundating him with remembrance, that soft masculine resonance will recall in an instant the warmth and courtesy of the South. Those unmistakable tones will surely elicit a smile and turn my head.

The next time you're sitting next to a gentleman of the South, listen closely and allow yourself to be embraced by the sound of his voice. I don't know why their voices are so beautiful. Maybe generations of listening to the cry of Negro spirituals influenced the very sound of southern men, or perhaps they simply don't have to howl over the din of big city traffic. Whatever the reason, the result is magnificent.

NEW YORK'S GLITTER faded as the subtle loveliness of Mississippi enveloped me.

I was willing to admit that the Gulf Coast had hidden treasures—like the sonorous sounds of the southern man's voice—but not for a long time to concede that a good thought had ever come out of the mind of a southern slaveholder. A museum helped me lose this prejudice. The impact was powerful because I didn't expect it.

At the beginning of February 1998, before my husband and I had actually met each other, we were enjoying daily telephone calls. I suppose I fell in love with that voice before I fell in love with the man. During one of our evening talks, he said, "We now have a presidential library." "Which president?" I asked. When he responded, "Jefferson Davis," I was amused. "Oh, yes, the first and only president of the Confederacy," I said, and dismissed it.

Like all American schoolchildren, I studied the Civil War. Our lessons included Jefferson Davis and his role as the father of the Confederacy. But we studied "the War of Rebellion" in a cursory manner. Upon moving to Ocean Springs, I was astounded to learn that some in this area still call that terrible conflict "the War of Northern Aggression," and even more astounded to find that some Union soldiers behaved very badly during that war. Had I received, even in liberal New York, a biased education? Was I given incomplete information?

The Jefferson Davis Presidential Library is located on the fifty-five-acre grounds of Beauvoir House, a handsome antebellum raised cottage on the Gulf in Biloxi, which Davis purchased after the war, and where he lived with his wife until his death in 1898. Since 1941, Beauvoir has been open to the public as a museum dedicated to Davis's memory. When I first glimpsed these places—before the ravages of

Katrina—they were the architectural jewels of Beach Boulevard, although Jefferson Davis himself was a shadowy figure. Their exquisite beauty first lured me there—the broad expanse of green and ancient live oak trees framing the main house with its two flanking cottages. Inside these buildings, among the many artifacts and personal items, I felt the presence of Jefferson Davis; these things inspired me to find out more about the man. I went back time and time again, and the once elusive figure emerged from the shadows with added dimensions that I had not known before. I discovered that Jefferson Davis was a man of many accomplishments totally unrelated to slavery.

In the words that follow, I barely touch upon the issue of slavery or Davis's slaveholding. But that's not because I'm glossing over slavery. Of course we're all appalled by this archaic institution. My purpose here is to point out that Jefferson Davis had some admirable qualities, even though he owned slaves and believed in the institution of slavery.

FOR MORE THAN THIRTY YEARS before Jefferson Davis became president of the Confederacy, he had distinguished careers in both the U.S. military and national politics. A West Point graduate, he formed, trained, and led the Mississippi Rifles in the Mexican-American War. Mississippi voters elected him to the U.S. House of Representatives, and for several years he served in the Senate of the United States. As a senator, he chaired the Military Affairs Committee, updated the army, worked diligently in defense of the frontier, and researched routes for the transcontinental railroad. President Franklin Pierce chose him as his secretary of war, and he served admirably.

Davis opposed federal interference in the affairs of individual states, on constitutional grounds, but he also vehemently opposed the South's secession from the Union and worked for years to avert secession. Less provincial than many of his southern brethren, Davis did not underestimate the likely, horrific ramifications of a civil war. Even after South Carolina seceded in 1860, Davis opposed secession and continued trying to mollify the enmity between the North and the South.

Reluctantly, in January 1861, Davis acceded to wishes of Mississippi state legislators, resigned his U.S. Senate seat, and announced the secession of Mississippi. His southern colleagues selected Davis for the presidency of the Confederacy in part because he was more moderate than his compatriots. As president, he appointed Judah P. Benjamin as attorney general of the Confederate States, the first Jew to hold such a high position in American government. He urged the development of manufacturing in the

South and wisely appointed Robert E. Lee as commander of the Army of Northern Virginia.

An expert commander and public servant, Davis had an extensive and noteworthy career. He was famous for his honesty and lived by a strict code of behavior regarding money, favors, and gifts. Misled though he was about slavery, he demonstrated the courage of his convictions throughout his life and gave unflinching encouragement to unpopular people and policies. He was a compelling speaker with a wealth of experience in public affairs and was well respected for his lucid reasoning.

Courage and loyalty were at the heart of Jefferson Davis's ethics, and when the South's inevitable defeat became apparent, he did not escape to Cuba or Europe. Captured and jailed for two years on charges of treason, he endured humiliating, though not cruel, treatment. A man of great pride, he declined to ask for an official pardon to reinstate his citizenship, preferring to live as an exile in his own country. Yet Davis never lost his dignity, his love for the South, nor his love of America.

Although Davis was unapologetic for supporting the institution of slavery, he believed slaves should be treated with respect, and he apparently acted according to his principles. A year before Davis died, he received a letter from one of his former slaves, his personal attendant, James H. Jones, who had enjoyed a prosperous career after his manumission. "I have always been as warmly attached to you as when I was your body servant," Jones wrote. Several years later another former slave, James Lucas, expressed fondness and admiration for Davis, saying, "He was quality."

After the war, Davis had to pick up the pieces of his life and begin anew; he chose Beauvoir as the place to do so. Now the people of this country face the challenge of giving new life to Davis's beautiful and historic Beauvoir after the ravages of Katrina. With federal funding, restoration and rebuilding has begun. Au revoir, Beauvoir. May you come back soon.

Pretty Women

THE NIGHT WAS HOT, and steamy in the way only New Orleans can be. Jerry and I were leaving a theatre where we had just watched *Gone with the Wind*. The sultry air heightened the heady sweetness of the night-blooming jasmine. I loved it.

"Do you regret that the feminine way women dressed in those times has vanished?" I asked.

He chuckled quietly and said, "No, because southern women still look that way."

We were walking to the car, and as I looked around at the other moviegoers in the parking lot, I saw what he saw. The women were dressed in silk chiffon and gauzy cotton dresses, some of them strapless, a couple with full skirts; all looked soft. One young woman even had a flower in her hair. In my omnipresent black top, classic black trousers, black ballet flats, and red lipstick, I was chic, of course, but I didn't look southern.

With even features and fine complexions, southern women are pretty. Mississippi, for example, has produced more Miss Americas per capita than any other state. But I don't believe the Almighty had a bias toward Mississippi; I think Mississippi women are pretty because they enjoy being pretty and know how to make themselves so, and because they're not afraid to be feminine. Courteous, well spoken, and goal oriented, even today's young southern career women haven't lost their femininity. Although wasp-waisted Scarlett O'Hara crinolines are no longer worn, the carry-over in wardrobe sensibility remains. There's stability in southern culture, and the careful observer will notice its expression in women's clothing. Neither the androgynous nor the preppy look has taken hold here. No "Boho" look either: the return of hippie style was never successful in this region. Fashion is more colorful and playful in the South—the festive Mardi Gras influence, perhaps. And southern women do love a bit of sparkle at night.

Unlike many women in this country, they don't neutralize their sexuality with their clothing. A friend in California, for example, who was pregnant with her baby girl, said, "I'm going to dress her in a gender-neutral way." Another L.A. friend, a smart, concerned mother, never gave her little girl a doll to play with, fearful that this might discourage the child from aiming for a profession later. Old-fashioned or not, women of the Deep South have an ingrained femininity and exult in their womanliness. They don't seem to care if you call them the chairman of the board, the chair, or the chairperson. They know that they are first, last, and always female. And they dress accordingly, and tastefully. They don't overstate their femininity with clothes that are too tight or too revealing. They emphasize their curves in subtle ways. Southern women know the appeal of a little mystery. And, for the record, southern ladies do not walk around barefoot!

Southern women are expected to be pretty and tasteful; they always have been. They still love beautiful fragrances and cosmetics. They still get dressed up for church on Sundays, even as church dress has become more casual elsewhere. They may be coolheaded about other topics, but not about their wardrobe and certainly not about their arsenal of beauty items. My friend Barbara, a pretty Louisiana native now residing in Texas, puts all her makeup in her carry-aboard bag when she packs for a flight, just in case her luggage gets lost in transit.

Southern women aim for charm, as opposed to hard chic. The haircut of the moment elsewhere may be stylishly short, but most of the women I see here wear it fairly long and full. If they're too mature for that, they wear shorter styles with movement, adding softness to their features. These women seem to recognize that classic good looks last forever. It's not that they resist change: they adapt the latest trends with their own soft southern accents. The result is a parade of good-looking women, dressed accordingly, maintaining a standard that's timeless and stylish. You see this standard everywhere on the Gulf Coast, especially among ladies who lunch.

Tantalizing aromas wafted from Mary Mahoney's kitchen. On the wall facing me was a very old copy of Rembrandt's *The Holy Family*, and I was taking pleasure in a meal of broiled snapper with my beautiful, blonde friend Merrill—a Mississippi belle if ever there was one. When a large party of older women arrived wearing hats, we paused to admire them. I recall one woman, a bit younger-looking than the others, who was very chic in a simple, wide-brimmed straw hat and neutral-colored sheath—a look reminiscent of Audrey Hepburn. Her bright red lipstick, probably "Fire and Ice" by Revlon, made for a stunning combination. Another lady wearing a black "pillbox" with her bangs peeking out and a simple strand of pearls reminded me of Jackie Kennedy Onassis, classic and completely pulled together. One brunette had on a more elaborate confection, a big, orchid hat with swirls of fabric—the type I'd expect to see at the Kentucky Derby—and a suit of the same delicate orchid color.

The scene evoked happy childhood memories for Merrill. "That reminds me so much of mah mama, when everyone wore a hat," she said.

Although I'm not enamored of hats and wear them only in cold climates, I admit that, properly worn, a hat adds mystery to a woman. Who can resist looking at a woman with a brim casting a shadow over her face? Don't you try to get a glimpse of her features? Look at classic Hollywood films from the 1930s and 40s. Such allure is missing in our jeans-and-T-shirt society, but southern women still have it.

Southern women don't debate style versus substance. They don't apologize for wanting to please men by dressing well. And they don't resent men for responding to a beautiful woman. Southern women know they are women; so they don't fight it. Just as their houses reflect their sense of beauty, their wardrobes are barometers of their joy in being a woman.

I MUST CONFESS that there's one aspect of southern womanhood I have yet to understand. I turn my attention to it now.

Football is a major pastime throughout the country, generating millions of dollars in revenue, but in the South, football assumes an entirely different status. The late Marino Casem, longtime football coach at Alcorn State University, who was called "the

Black Godfather of Mississippi," once described the difference:

In the East, football is a cultural exercise. On the West Coast, it is a tourist attraction. In the Midwest, it is cannibalism. But in the South, it is a religion, and Saturday is the holy day.

I accept his regional distinctions. They're brilliant. But there's a profound truth about football in the South that I doubt the coach ever gave a moment's thought: even the women down here love football!

Yes, it's true. Southern women are as immersed in football as the men are. I have seen sweet, feminine, otherwise normal women—southern belles, even— bellow, "Sooie! Sooie! Sooie!" at the top of their lungs.

Never once, before I moved to Mississippi, had I experienced this peculiar phenomenon. Southern women care passionately about this sport. They're crazy about football!

Why southern women are football fanatics will forever remain a mystery to me. (I try not to think about it.)

Tastes of the South

"**S**ATsumas! Get yo' SATsumas!" the mustachioed vendor cried on Carrolton Street in New Orleans. I pulled up behind his truck and admired the arrangement of fruits and vegetables, colorful in the midday sun. Although it was November, this was another one of those scorching days, the kind that melts the tube of lipstick I always keep in the console of my car. To stop for fresh farm produce was the perfect antidote. But what on earth are satsumas? What are mirlitons? And Vidalia onions?

I hopped out of my car and, curious as ever, asked the vendor with the bristling mustache, "Where are the satsumas and what are they?" He told me they're a lot like clementines because they are seedless. So I immediately bought some. (I've since learned that they're grown commercially in south Louisiana and other southern states and ripen in the fall. They were introduced to the United States in Florida in 1876 from Japan, which is still the center of the satsuma industry.)

And mirlitons? I'd heard of Tchaikovsky's "Dance of the Mirlitons" from *The Nutcracker Suite*, but that mirliton is a toy flute resembling a kazoo, about the size and shape of a cigar, certainly not edible. The vegetable mirliton grows in southern Louisiana on a climbing vine. I suppose it does look a bit like a flute. I discovered that it tastes like eggplant crossed with an avocado. Paul Prudhomme and nonprofessional Louisiana cooks stuff and season mirlitons the same ways they stuff eggplants.

Vidalia onions were my favorite find of the day. I love these Georgia onions because they're much milder and sweeter than other onions I've eaten. We used to get them only in the spring, but modern technology now makes them available most of the year. (The name "Vidalia Onions" is trademarked and, according to Georgia law, only onions grown in certain counties in Georgia can be called "Vidalias." Their taste supposedly is related to the amount of sulphur in the soil there.)

Luckily, my chance meeting at the food truck happened very early in my southern experience. This encounter piqued my appetite as much as restaurant dining did. Now I could experiment at home with these unfamiliar ingredients and create my own specialties. And I'd be able to join in the food discussions, too. Elated by my discovery, I hurried home with my exotic treasures.

Arriving back in Mississippi, I rolled down my car windows and inhaled the aroma of brewed coffee wafting in the air. The scent was so enticing that I followed my nose and walked right into an Ocean Springs restaurant. Chattering diners, clinking glasses and silverware, and the polite inquiries of waiters filled the place. In the courtyard, sparrows hopped about expectantly, cocking their heads, and looking for crumbs from the delectable locally baked baguettes. One blue jay was so confident in our midst that I felt I ought to offer him butter for his bread.

I ordered lunch, first looking around to see what other diners were eating. At the neighboring table, someone was eating a slice of pecan pie and persuaded me to have one. Normally I don't have dessert, but I found myself deriving enormous unalloyed pleasure from each morsel. I had become as hedonistic as the Mississippians. It felt good.

Since my first days in the state, I've discovered that Mississippi's culinary heritage is rich, both literally and figuratively: creamed okra and corn, creamy cheese grits, old-time buttermilk pie, sweet potato pie, pecan pie, peach cobbler, applesauce cookies. And sweetened iced tea—known simply as "sweet tea"—with everything, regardless of season. While

Mississippi has adapted to contemporary standards by offering "smart" choices on restaurant menus, the delectable food of their Anglo and African ancestors still reigns supreme.

Bacon grease, for example, is the indispensable ingredient in southern cooking, especially for seasoning vegetables. Initially used by poor people, bacon grease can infuse a simple vegetable with mouthwatering flavor, making it popular to this day among even upscale southern cooks. Many southerners save the grease that's left in the skillet after they cook bacon and keep it in a coffee can or glass jar. It was a real shocker when I first learned that! But in time I found that green beans do have more flavor when cooked in a little bacon grease. The use of bacon grease would have been anathema to me, but now that we're all more aware of the differences between hydrogenated oils and trans fatty acids, it doesn't bother me as much.

IF YOU ENJOY FINE DINING and have been spoiled by living in the world capital, you can become jaded by the multitude of dining choices. There are twenty thousand restaurants in New York. After sampling the best of international cuisine, your taste buds become apathetic. At least mine did. And so I was blasé when I approached the southern table. Anyway, with my urban background, I always fancied myself as "too chic to eat."

I first heard the term "white trash food" from a Texan, a nice young lady living in Beverly Hills. She was referring to potato chips, corn chips, and all those edibles that come in bags, which are high in calories and low in nutrition. I dislike the term "white trash"—it's unkind—but her comment somehow stirred a bit of prejudice in me. Since "white trash" often refers to poor people, and southern food originated with poor southerners, I reasoned that all southern food must be junk food. How wrong I was! I've come to admire the inventiveness of Mississippians and the simple country cooking of their ancestors, which continues today and is nothing short of delicious. More than once I've heard the phrase, "my mother was a fine country woman."

Snobbery about food notwithstanding, I've always had a healthy appetite, so I wasn't able to resist the temptations of Mississippi or Louisiana dishes for long. When I was newly married, I cooked out of a low-fat cookbook in an attempt to keep my husband healthy. But, as much as he appreciated my concern and efforts, the result was that he took me out to eat virtually every night, and this made me very happy. It never occurred to me that he was in despair, unable to look at yet another piece of undressed romaine lettuce or thinly sliced cucumber.

Once initiated into the joys of real southern cookery, oh, what wonders there were. Sometimes the discovery was practical—better to eat a satsuma than a tangerine because you don't have to struggle with a tight skin and there are no seeds. Most often, though, there were gustatory delights. I had never eaten shrimp étouffée. Boy! How could shrimp and bell peppers and celery and green onions and who knows what else produce something so mouthwateringly delicious? When I discovered that fried chicken tasted different in Mississippi (I still don't know why it does), I adopted another dish that I had disdained to eat before. And who knew that Cajun and Creole cooking were different? Wasn't everything just blackened?

The history of Cajun and Creole food fascinates me. As I understand it, Creole food descends from the wealthy white French people who originally settled New Orleans and the Gulf Coast. It is closer to its European roots than Cajun food is, and includes many rich sauces adapted from classic French ones. Creole food is served in old-line New Orleans restaurants like Galatoire's and Commander's Palace. Cajun food is heartier fare, tracing its roots to the French Canadians (Acadians) who settled the rural region west and south of New Orleans after the British kicked them out of Nova Scotia. One-pot meals like gumbo, crawfish étouffée, and jambalaya are Cajun creations. But over the years, Cajun and Creole foods have cross-pollinated, and both have been influenced by the food traditions of African

Americans, Native Americans, Caribbeans, Germans, Spanish, Italians, and others who have migrated to south Louisiana.

Every home cook will benefit if she has at least one gumbo and jambalaya in her repertoire, and there are infinite varieties of each. They're reliable dishes, because you can't really ruin either one of them. They allow for creativity and therefore for mistakes. When in doubt, I keep adding Tabasco™. Sometimes my guests have turned an alarming shade of crimson, but they have all survived.

Tabasco, a staple in southern kitchens, is one of this area's culinary inventions. About the time of the Civil War, Louisiana native Edmund McIllhenny obtained some Mexican capsicum peppers. He was enthusiastic about their ability to enliven the taste of plain food, so he planted the seeds on Avery Island in Louisiana and started to create variations of a hot sauce, finally settling in 1868 on the recipe you find in the stores today. McIllhenny's descendants still grow the peppers and make Tabasco sauce.

Gumbo is the perfect dish to serve a large group. It takes a long time, but the results are well worth the wait. "First, you make a roux." I can't count the times I've heard that phrase since I've lived here. Gumbo, and many other Cajun and Creole dishes begin with the roux, which makes everything taste better. Roux is equal parts of white flour and butter, oil, or pork fat, cooked very slowly over low heat and stirred constantly, to keep it from burning, until it reaches the desired shade of brown (specified in recipes as the color of peanut butter, brown paper bag, pecan shell, or dark brown sugar). Patience is essential.

IN SPITE OF the enormous changes in the American food consciousness in the past twenty-five years that have resulted in increasingly sophisticated palates, a generic quality characterizes the mainstream foods of our nation. When you travel across the United States, you're faced with menus that are almost completely interchangeable, and you'll look down the list of desserts and invariably find apple pie, blueberry pie, cherry pie, and vanilla ice cream. There's nothing wrong with that, but it doesn't offer excitement.

In Germany, a friend said to me, "There's no real American cuisine, nothing that belongs to you alone." Groping for an answer, I considered burgers, fries, ketchup—foods that speak Americana—but they weren't impressive. The only significant food that's distinctively American, I decided at the time, is turkey at Thanksgiving. But that was before I moved to the Mississippi Gulf Coast.

The foods here offer incredible variety. They draw not only upon traditional southern (soul) food, but also Cajun and Creole foods. There are so many locally grown fruits and vegetables and, of course, fabulous fresh seafood. The blend of all these traditions is the unmistakable stamp of Gulf Coast cuisine. Consider these local specialties: cheese straws, barbecued meatballs, fried chicken wings, sweet potato chips, deviled eggs, crawfish pies, marinated shrimp, oyster puffs, muffuletta canapés, clam dip, hot crawfish dip, barbecued shrimp, crab claws, venison meatballs, duck gumbo, Mississippi mud pie, pralines, and watermelon rind pickles!

Mississippi homegrown watermelon is in a class by itself!

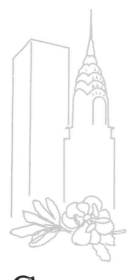

Katrina

SLENDER, WHITE, and oddly graceful egrets used to fish contentedly on the bayou in front of our house. They were gone now. I listened for the mysterious "ooh-hoo" of the owl, but dead silence was all I heard. Where had all the seagulls gone and what were they doing now? And the mallards, with their iridescent necks—they must have been at such a loss.

It was the first time we had been allowed entry onto our property, just four days after the storm. Our house and the others in our cul-de-sac had left barely a trace. The oak and pecan and magnolia and mimosa trees had dematerialized. We walked amid the wreckage in dazed grief.

WE HAD KNOWN KATRINA would be bad, but no one anticipated the unprecedented magnitude of the destruction. On Saturday night, two days before

Hurricane Katrina struck, Jerry and I were having dinner with Lucy Denton and her two adorable daughters, Dawn and Drew, at the Palace Hotel and Casino's Mignon's, an excellent restaurant known for its steak. The waiter advised us that the restaurant would close early for storm preparation. We were still discussing the pros and cons of evacuating the next day, hoping the storm would change course. Everyone I knew on the Coast had the same thought, "We'll be back on Tuesday."

Katrina made landfall on Monday, August 29, 2005. Jerry and I had left town the day before, to stay with friends in Hattiesburg. We lived away from the Coast for most of the year after that, residing primarily in Fairhope—a pretty little town. Jerry was working nearby in Mobile, Alabama. I drove to Ocean Springs about four times a week to search through the debris for anything personal I could find. After about six months, I gave up the search reluctantly: it was time to let go.

After that year away, Jerry and I returned to the Coast to find a place to live. We had decided not to rebuild; we would look for a house in Gulfport, close to Jerry's office—someplace that was "high and dry." As much as we loved our Ocean Springs property and the calming view of the bayou, I couldn't bear to live on the water again. With so many of our neighbors now living elsewhere, it wouldn't be the same anyway.

I STARTED DRIVING WEST from Biloxi on Highway 90; its beauty had always made it my preferred route. Once a major artery, there was almost no traffic on this road now, a whole year after the storm. I had difficulty orienting myself, as the markers I had depended on had disappeared. Naked land was all around me. The desolate landscape was a mirror of my soul.

My heart ached as I passed where Green Oaks once stood. I remembered the string quartet that played on my wedding day, when we were full of hope and joy. Anxiously, I approached Beauvoir. The small cottage known as the library pavilion (where Jefferson Davis wrote his epic *The Rise and Fall of the Confederate Government*) had been obliterated, as had the Hayes Cottage and the Confederate Soldier's Museum. They would never be there again. The main house itself and the presidential library sustained major damage. I was thankful that I had wandered many times through Beauvoir, and its outbuildings and grounds, always sharing the experience with out-of-town friends.

Aah, Mary Mahoney's, the Old French Restaurant, had reopened! There had always been a watermark on the wall of the restaurant to indicate how high Hurricane Camille's waters rose. Now there was a new watermark for Katrina, and it was eight feet higher. The survival of this familiar gathering place for Coastal residents comforted me, and I kept driving.

Insistent images of my old Mississippi Gulf Coast

took shape in my mind's eye: gorgeous, white-columned Chimneys Restaurant, where my friend Jolie and I celebrated her engagement over lunch, surrounded by camellia trees; Tullis-Toledano Manor, where she married David in a beautiful ceremony; and the Denton House, site of so much laughter and lively conversation. The Biloxi–Ocean Springs Bridge, which I traversed daily, had felt like my backyard.

The sky was becoming leaden now, and clouds hung oppressively low. I passed a sign whose rusted frame hung half off its moorings. The base was corroded, surrounded by drooping bushes, and its top was broken off. A white flag flapped in the wind against the charcoal sky. It was inscribed with a phone number in red letters, a remnant of someone's business, I suppose. Where were they now?

A sign warning me of the 45 mph speed limit leaned so far to the right that I was amazed it was still standing. A little farther down, a billboard read, "IHOP Restaurant–Open 24 Hours," but its message was irrelevant. In front, a bright lemon-yellow fire hydrant listed to the left, half out of the ground. Everything was askew. Trees with only a few brown leaves remaining were dead and gnarled. I drove farther west, only to see more amputated trees, dry overgrown grass, and anemic, stunted palms. The battered old grass looked like tumbleweed, the wind whipping it up now. I wasn't used to seeing tumbleweed in lush green Mississippi; tumbleweed belonged to the West and cowboys. It had no place here.

Suddenly I came upon a cheerful signboard that looked like a 1950s ad for the French Riviera, with red letters informing me that this was the Biloxi Beach Resort. Superimposed on an illustration of an orange sky against blue white-capped water, the festive red script summoned the drivers on Highway 90 to stop right there and come on in. But underneath this sunny symbol, a faded turquoise metal frame on two tarnished poles was all that remained. Metal scraps were everywhere, littering the ground.

The Olive Garden restaurant sign, too, had withstood the storm, but the restaurant was gone. I remembered how long and patiently we all waited to get in, willing to stand in line because we all loved the view of the water, the salad, and garlic bread. And because it was fun to wait in that line. With Italian music playing in the background and Dean Martin crooning that the "moon hits your eye like a big pizza pie," and friendly people up and down the line to talk to, whether you knew them or not, the wait was a social occasion.

Moving on, I saw what was left of some new condos completed not long before Katrina let all hell break loose. Only skeletal wooden poles remained, like a haunting community of the dead. In Mississippi, the death toll was 250, with more people still unidentified or missing.

And so it went. Mile after mile, the destruction repeated its sad refrain. I drove to Pass Christian. I was grateful to have known this singularly lovely place before the storm's thirty-three-foot surges robbed us of so much history and beauty. But it broke my heart. The pitiful remains of Bay St. Louis, where ten- and twenty-block areas had not a single home left standing, were more than I could bear, at least not yet. I made a U-turn and headed back to Biloxi.

IT'S FUNNY—strange, I mean—how you get used to things. Shock gives way to surprise. Then depression becomes the norm. Acceptance comes much later.

IT HAS BEEN A DARK, dark time. But here suffering and resurrection go hand in hand.

AND THE BILOXI light-house stands.

Afterword

MANY OF THE PLACES I have written about exist only in memory now. Bridges have broken, buildings have collapsed, trees have died, and photographs have molded. But the qualities of the Mississippi people that I love—the friendliness, the manners, the love of beauty, the joy of sharing good food and just being together—these are intact. Not even the worst hurricane ever can destroy them. The southern spirit is ever optimistic, the southern heart warm. And memory strengthens everyone here.

And so they rebuild. For many, this was not their first hurricane. Some old-timers are rebuilding for the third time. Others have bought new houses near their old homes. Still others, less fortunate, make their shaky trailers as snug as they can.

NEARLY TWO YEARS have passed since Katrina ripped through here and forever changed the Mississippi Gulf Coast. The debris is gone. Most of the casinos are doing business again, and others are under construction. The Bay St. Louis Bridge opened in May, and construction has finally begun on a new bridge between Biloxi and Ocean Springs. The hair and manicure salons are buzzing; the southern belles are back to normal again. Real estate values continue to rise.

One recent morning, on the way to our new house in Gulfport, I drove by an elementary school yard where children were laughing and playing—so full of life—reminding me that a couple of years is "a long time" when you're eight years old. I was touched, but I moved on. I am not young, I reminded myself. Arriving at home, I pulled the car up beside my house and reflected on the children and the hurricane, my own life, and the passing of time. Just then, my neighbor's azalea bush caught my eye. Overnight it had slipped into its hot-pink spring dress.

It was the first day of March, and my world was new again.

Acknowledgments

MY WARM THANKS to Barney and Gwen McKee, my publishers at Quail Ridge Press, for their initial belief in this project.

Deepest thanks to JoAnne Prichard Morris, who has patiently clarified the text with her abundant recommendations.

The staff at Quail Ridge Press assisted me in numerous ways as I navigated the baffling terrain of placing my first book on the market. Marlana Walters worked unfailingly on the marketing strategies and acted as a diplomat when she handled the complicated aspects of the author's wishes versus publishing realities. Dana Walker thought through the sales tactics and possible venues and helped immeasurably with her professionalism. Cyndi Clark labored assiduously as I requested one design change after another. Terresa Ray answered my questions quickly and accurately, always willing to help in any way she could.

I'm grateful to Carmen Fulford, an artist living on the Mississippi Gulf Coast, for her interior illustrations.

This book owes a debt to Lucy Denton, who was my first reader and offered encouragement. I thank

Anne Jordan, who suggested that my observations about Mississippi would be feasible as a book. Special thanks to Jolie Machado, who urged me to write when I was still quite new to the Gulf Coast. Thanks to Dr. Sybil Estess, who read the original manuscript.

Conventional wisdom tells us that we are fortunate if we can count our true friends on one hand. Then I suffer from the embarrassment of riches. I can never be grateful enough for the friendships that I've enjoyed over the years. I do not list your names here for fear of accidentally omitting someone, but you know who you are. You have all been staunch allies in my life.

And of course, my deepest thanks to my husband Jerry, whose support is boundless.